THE OFFICIAL LEGO® ANNUAL 2018

CONTENTS

STOLEN CARS

The LEGO® CITY police are speaking to four crooks about some stolen cars. The crooks say they were only borrowing the cars. A likely story! Look at the picture below to find out which crook took which car. Then write the answers on the opposite page.

101552-B1

POLICE

A

B

C

D

ROADWORKS

These LEGO CITY road-builders are hard at work, making some new streets. Look at the five little pictures opposite and circle any that don't belong in the big picture.

60152

LEGO CITY

PN60152

A

B

C

D

E

7

ROCKY ROAD

This dune buggy is about to drive through some tricky terrain. Help the driver find his way through the winding paths between the rocks.

START

FINISH

LEGO CITY

9

OFF DUTY

This coast guard rescue team needs to cool off a bit . . . with some delicious ice cream! Look at all the flavours in the menu and then colour the scoops according to the colour key.

KEY

FLYING OVER THE SEA

This brave pilot is enjoying zooming around in his stunt plane above the waves in LEGO CITY harbour. But only one set of bricks opposite belongs to his plane. Can you circle the right set?

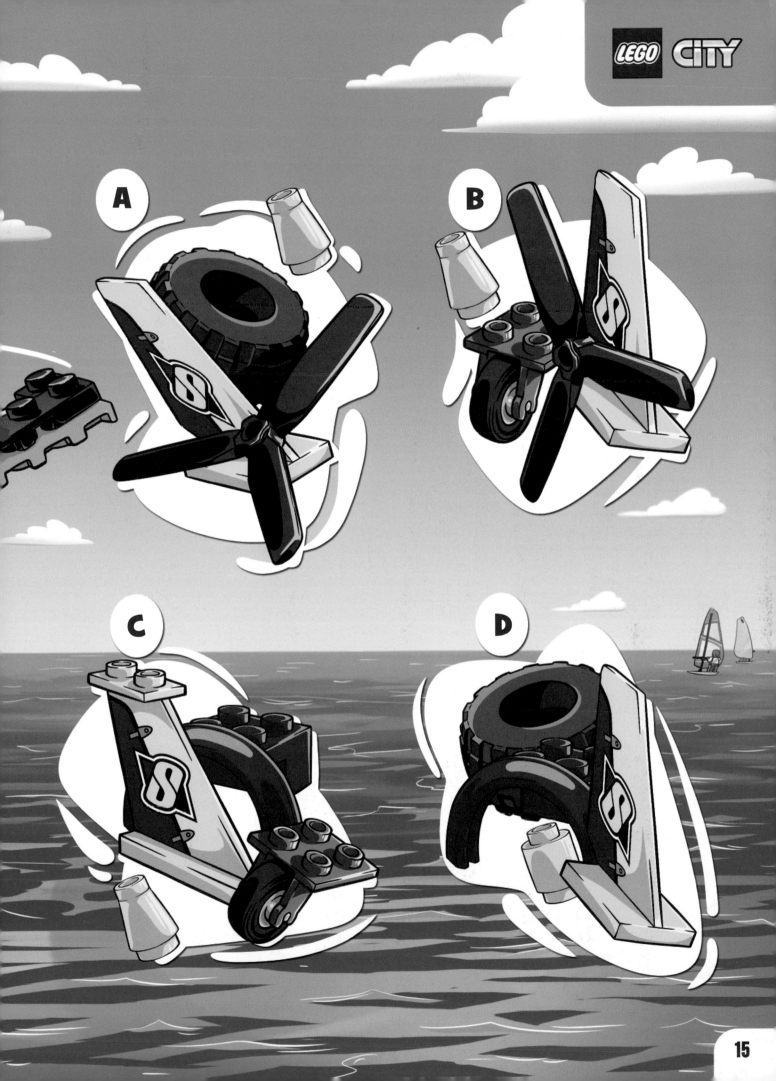

A

B

C

D

JUNGLE RESCUE

This explorer vehicle has broken down in the heart of the jungle. You need to help start it up again! Connect the cables so that the symbols at each end match. Hurry up . . . there is still so much to explore!

PIZZA TIME!

What kind of pizza will the delivery girl be carrying today? Use your colouring pencils and pens to create your own pizza toppings!

18

PRECIOUS CARGO

This truck driver has some important cargo to deliver in LEGO CITY. Look at the symbols the driver is thinking of below. Then match them with the symbols on the map to find two places where he must stop.

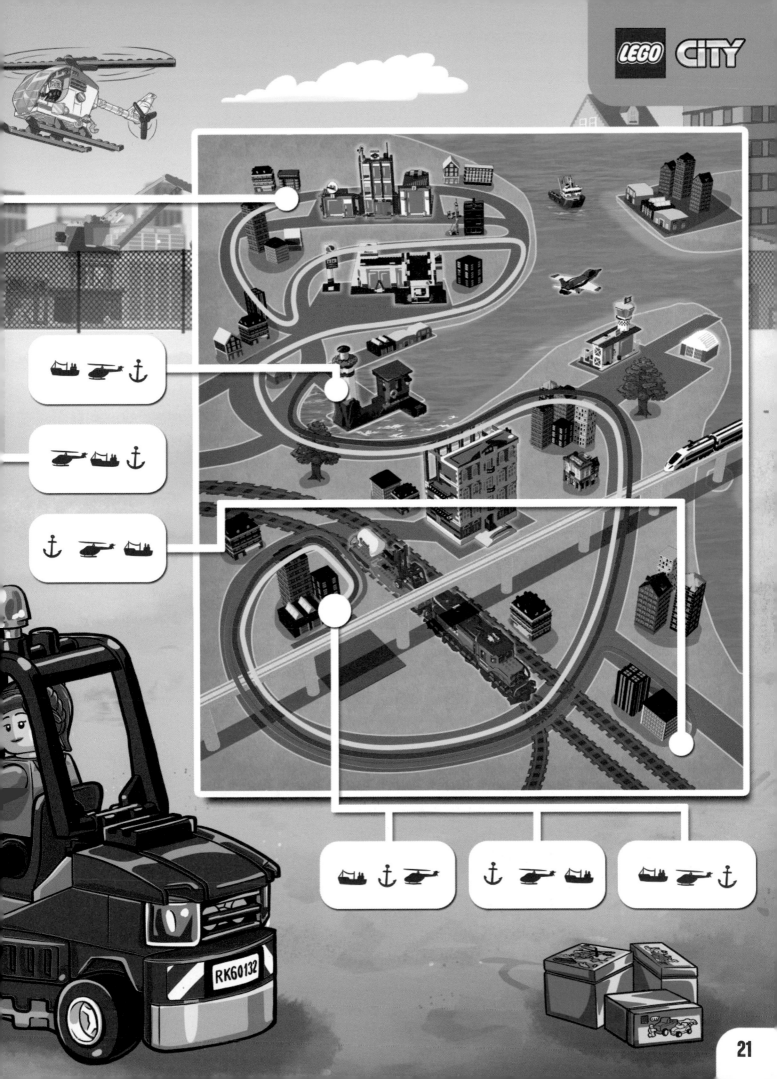

LET THE PATROL BEGIN!

The daytime coast guards are sailing their boats to your left, back to shore. The night-time coast guards are sailing their boats to your right, out to sea. Can you work out who is who by labelling each boat using the direction key on the opposite page?

KEY

L

R

23

SNOW BATTLE

The fresh snowfall is a great reason to start a snowball fight.
Untangle the lines to find out who threw each snowball.

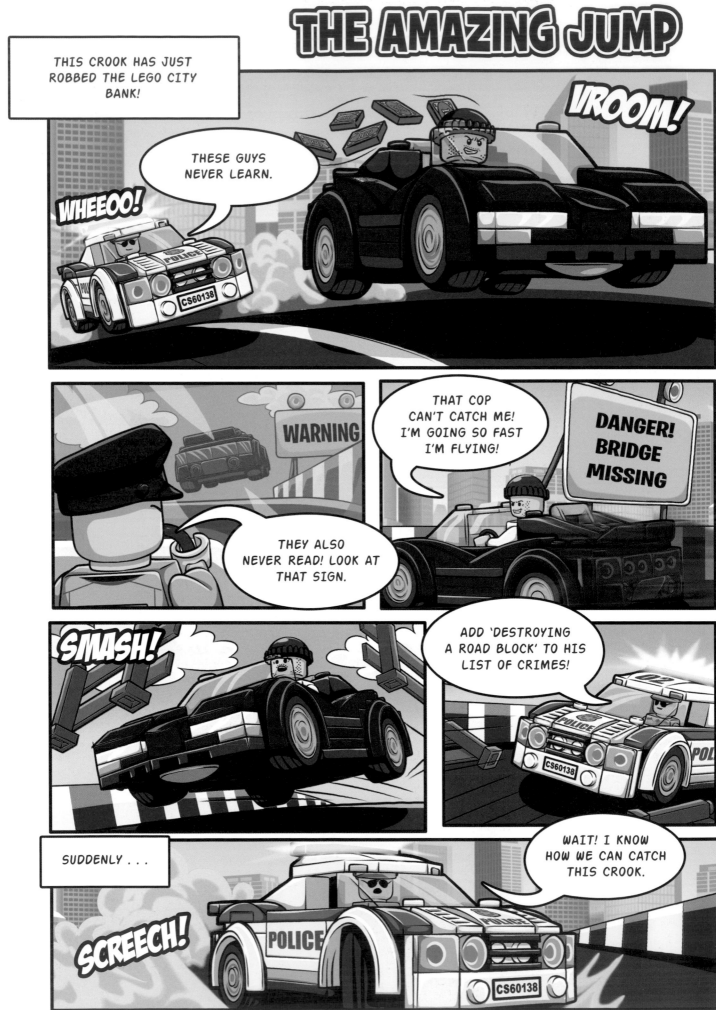

JUNGLE MISSION

A group of scientists is searching for wild animals in the thick jungle. Circle all the weird and wonderful creatures you can spot in the picture. There are sixteen to find.

ODD ONE OUT

Someone doesn't quite belong in each of the four photos below! Can you spot the odd one out each time? The symbols in the boxes give you a clue about what all the other minifigures in each group have in common.

BALLOONS, ANYONE?

Look at all Banana Guy's yellow, blue and orange balloons! Colour in the biggest balloon below with the colour you think there is most of. Then colour in the smallest balloon with the colour you think there is least of. Finally, colour in the middle balloon using the colour that is left.

THE MAZE OF FEAR

Do you dare to enter the Maze of Fear? Just remember to avoid the frightening things shown in the hint box. Draw the path that Spooky Boy should take to find his way out of the maze.

START

THAT'S MINE!

Match the objects with their owners. The symbols below should help you with this task! Keep in mind that every object symbol is made of two parts.

Greeble Trail

N

CHILLING POWERS

The Ice Queen has just frozen this whole castle with one swing of her magic icicle sword! Can you spot seven differences between the picture of the castle and its reflection in the lake?

CYBORG ARMY

This army of Cyborgs is almost complete! Only two more figures need to be put together. To finish the figures, write the letter of each Cyborg part in the correct circle on the two outlines below.

A

B

C

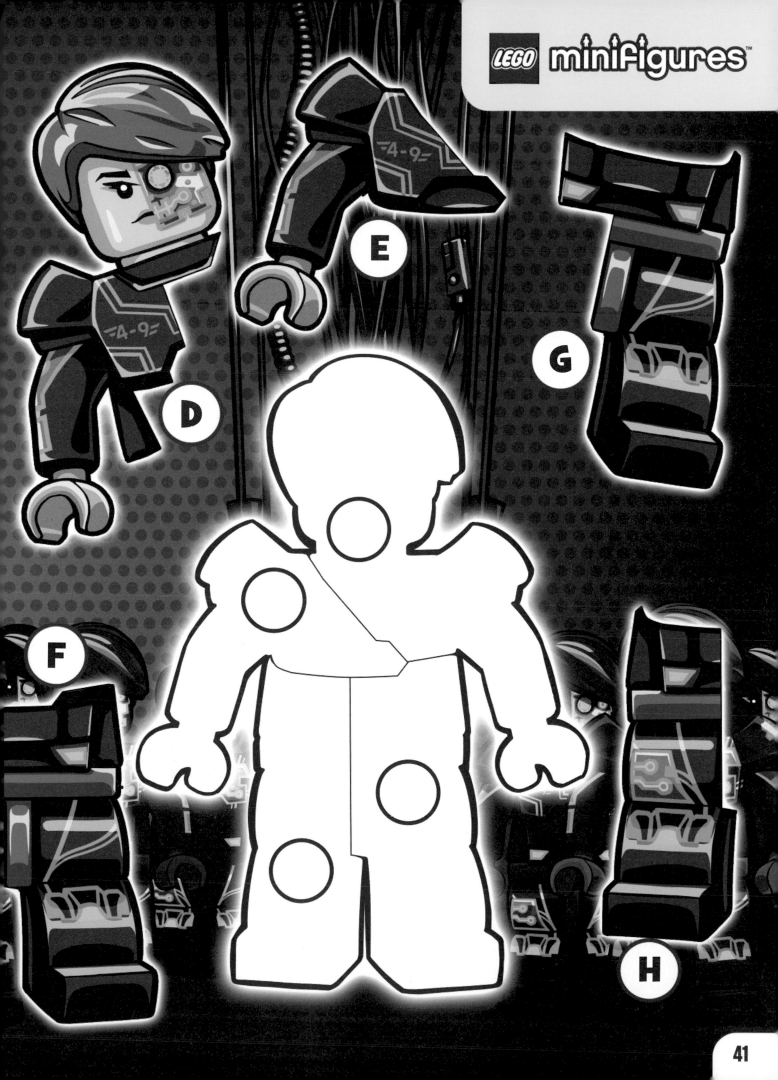

DESERT DOMINOES

This chain of dominoes has been built by the Desert Warrior, but it is missing a few tiles. Complete it with tiles by matching the end colours. The pieces you can use are at the bottom of the page – write the number of the ones you choose in the missing tile spaces. Good luck!

1   2   3   4

5

6

43

TARGET PRACTICE!

This is a game for you and a friend. Take it in turns to use your finger to hit the centre of the target . . . with your eyes closed! You both get three tries. Who gets the closest?

UNCHARTED TERRITORY

The Hiker's map is almost empty! Fill it in with drawings of mountains, rivers or whatever you like. Then follow Scallywag Pirate's directions to find the real treasure among the fake ones.

SUPER SPY

This clever security guard has spotted the Spy breaking into the garden of a house! But which of the shadows on the wall matches the Spy's silhouette? Draw a circle around the right one.

SPOOKY SLEEP

51

PARK WORKOUT

The Kickboxer has gone to the park to train before her next big fight.
Help her get through the hedge maze and reach the finish.
Ready? GO!

START

FINISH

DISAPPEARING NOTES

The Mariachi won't be able to play these tunes on his guitar if you don't help him. Look at the musical notes in every row below and work out how they repeat. Continue the pattern for each row.

1

2

3

ANSWERS

pp. 4-5

D

C

A

B

pp. 6-7

C

E

pp. 8-9

pp. 12-13

pp. 14-15: B

56

pp. 16-17

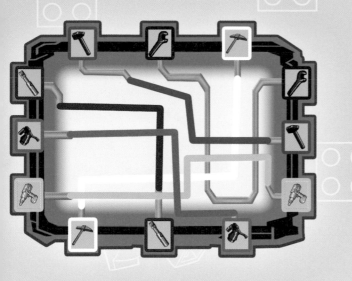

pp. 20-21

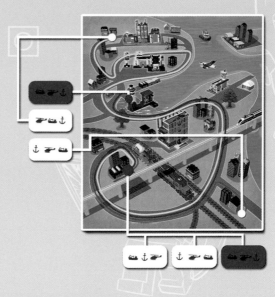

pp. 22-23

pp. 24-25

pp. 28-29

p. 30-31

pp. 32-33

pp. 34-35

pp. 36-37

pp. 38-39

pp. 40-41

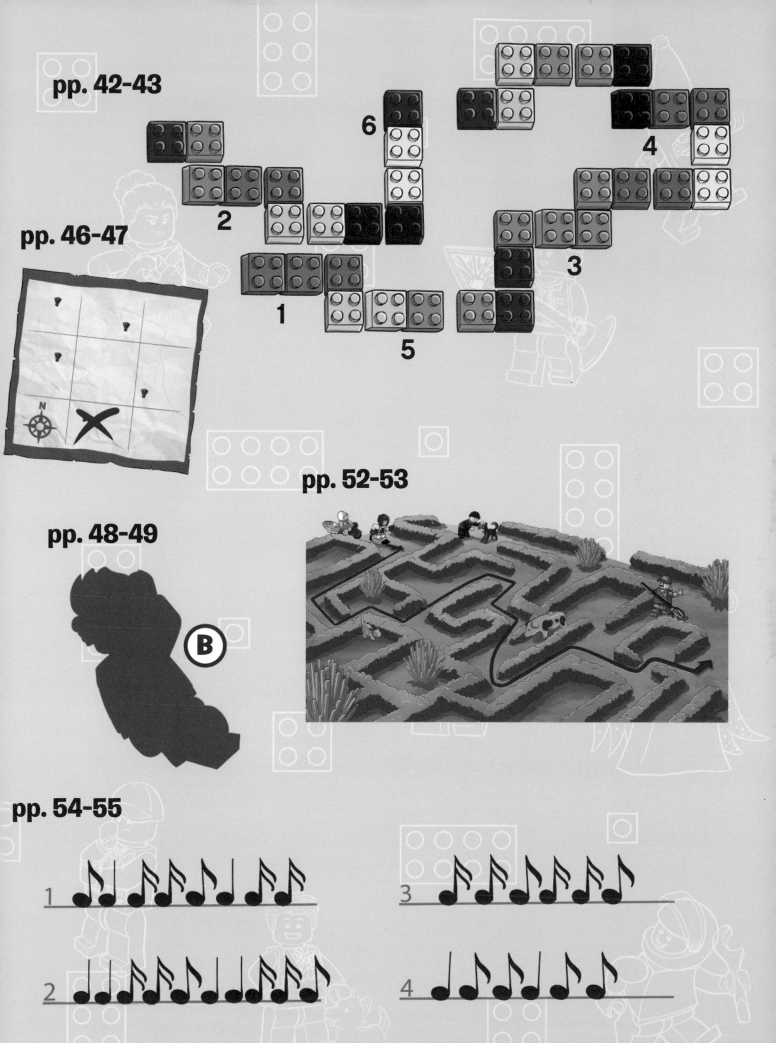

pp. 42-43

6

4

2

pp. 46-47

3

1

5

pp. 52-53

pp. 48-49

B

pp. 54-55

1

2

3

4

BUILD YOUR MINIFIGURE

Use your LEGO pieces and follow the steps shown to build your own minifigure.

SEE YOU LATER!